At the Supermarket

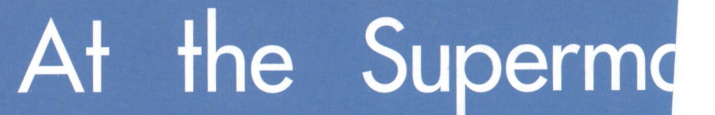

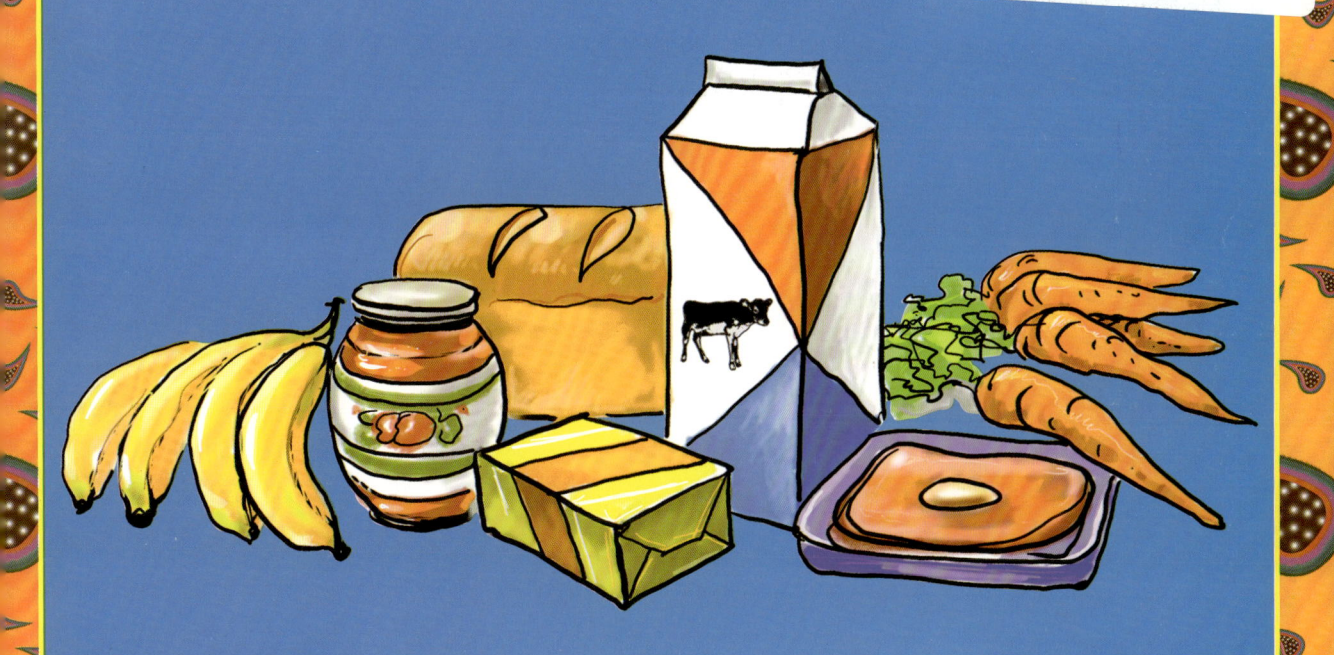

Written by Cory Winesap
Illustrated by Elena Petrov

We get the milk.

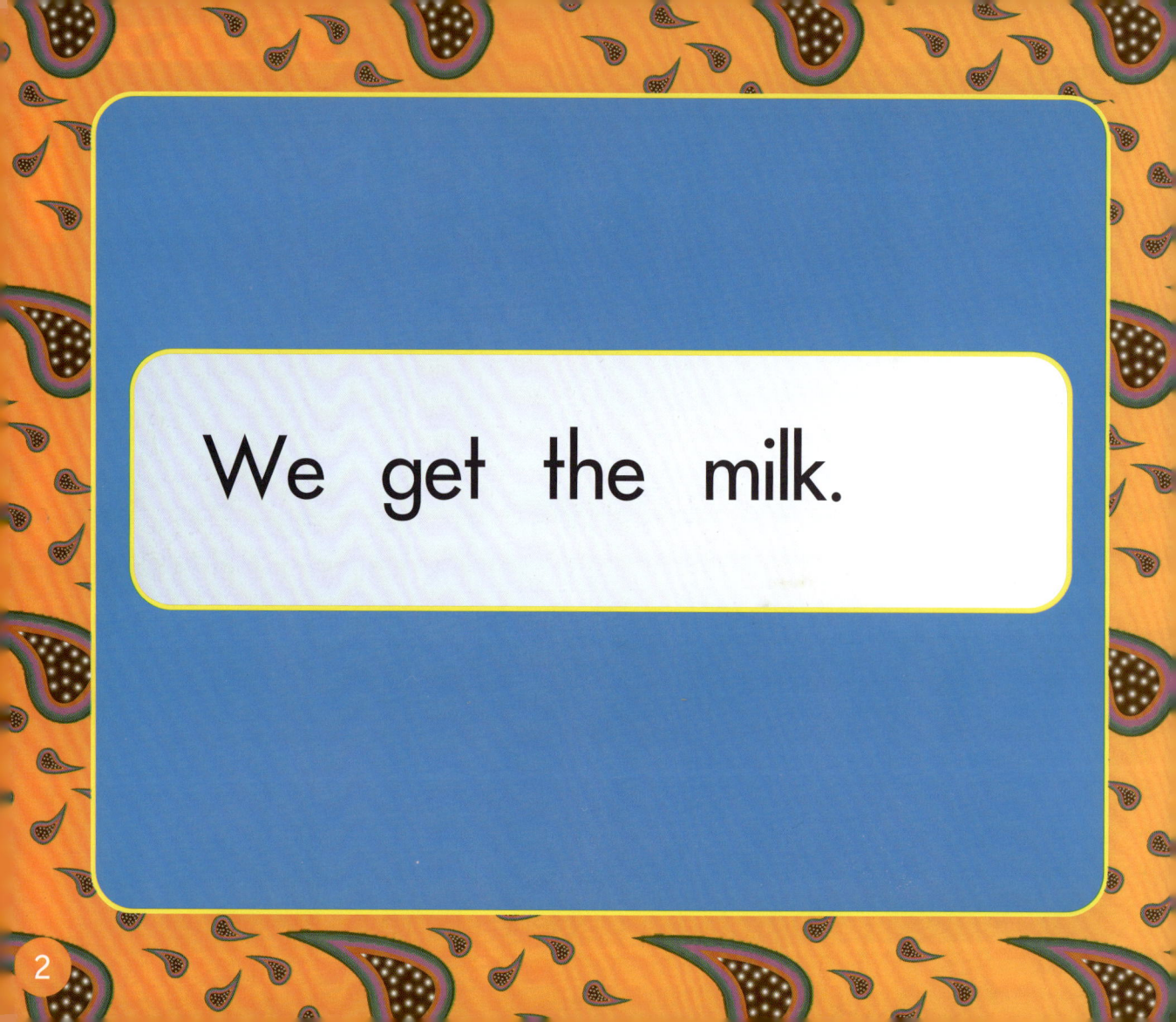

3

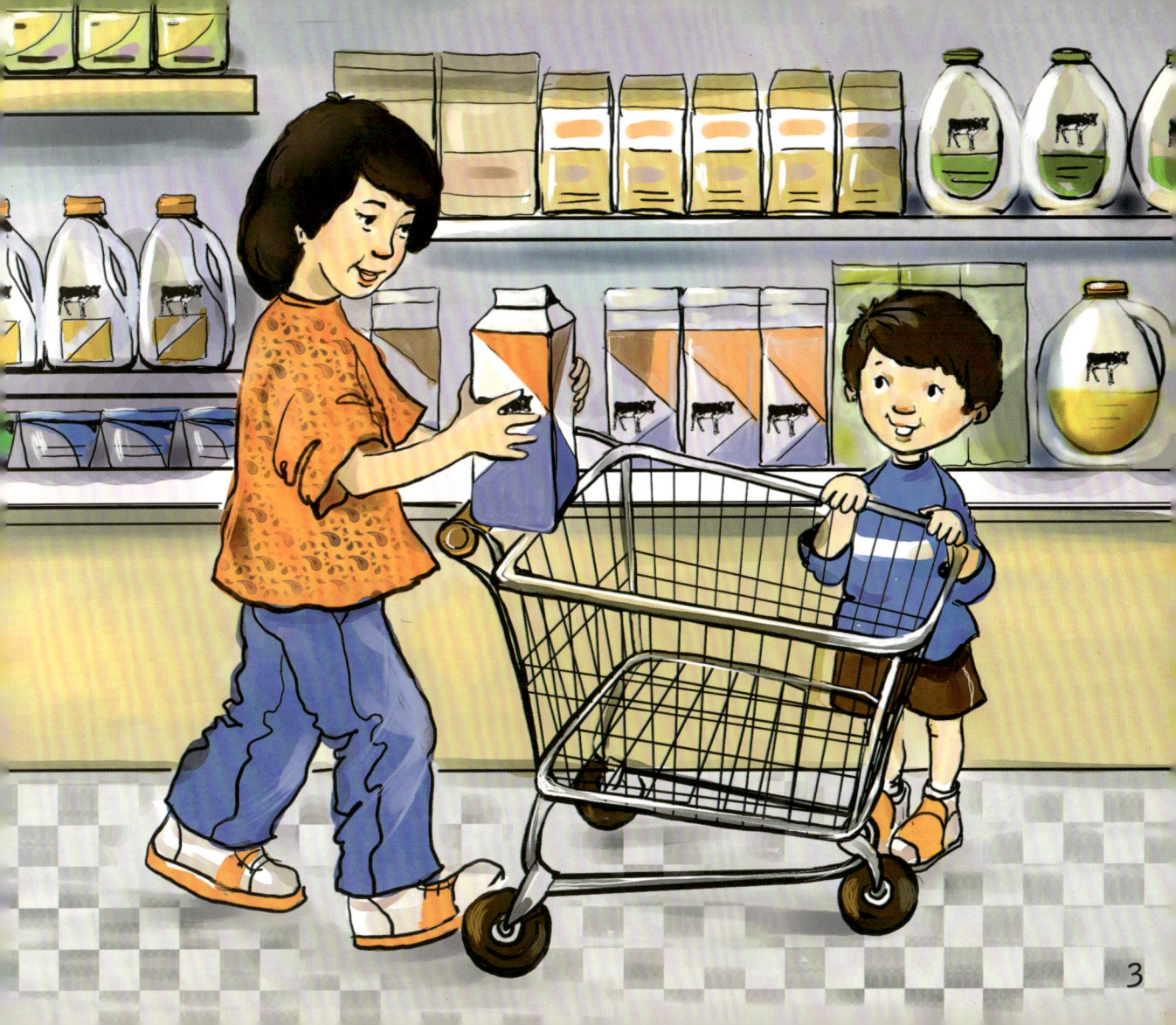

We get the butter.

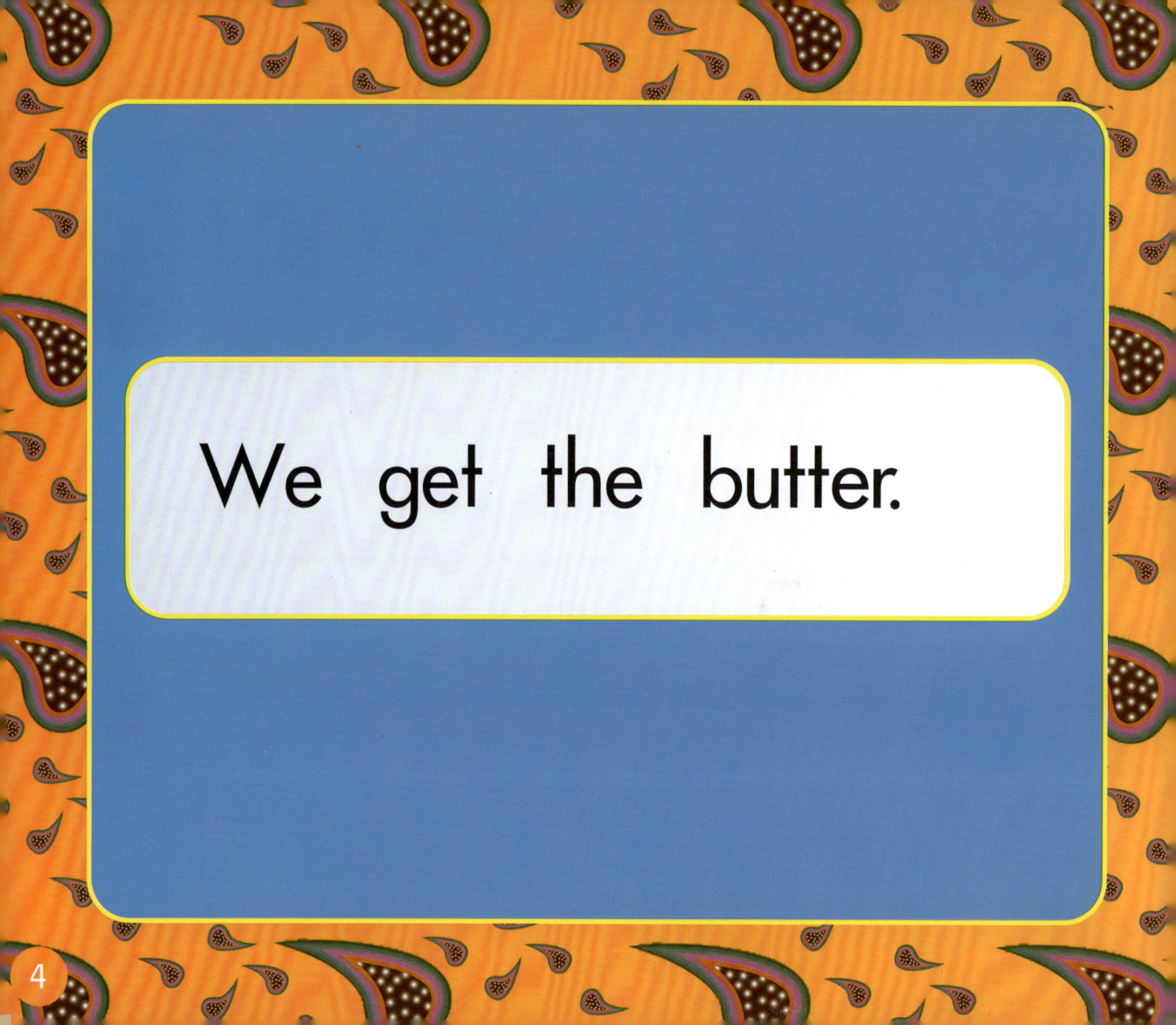

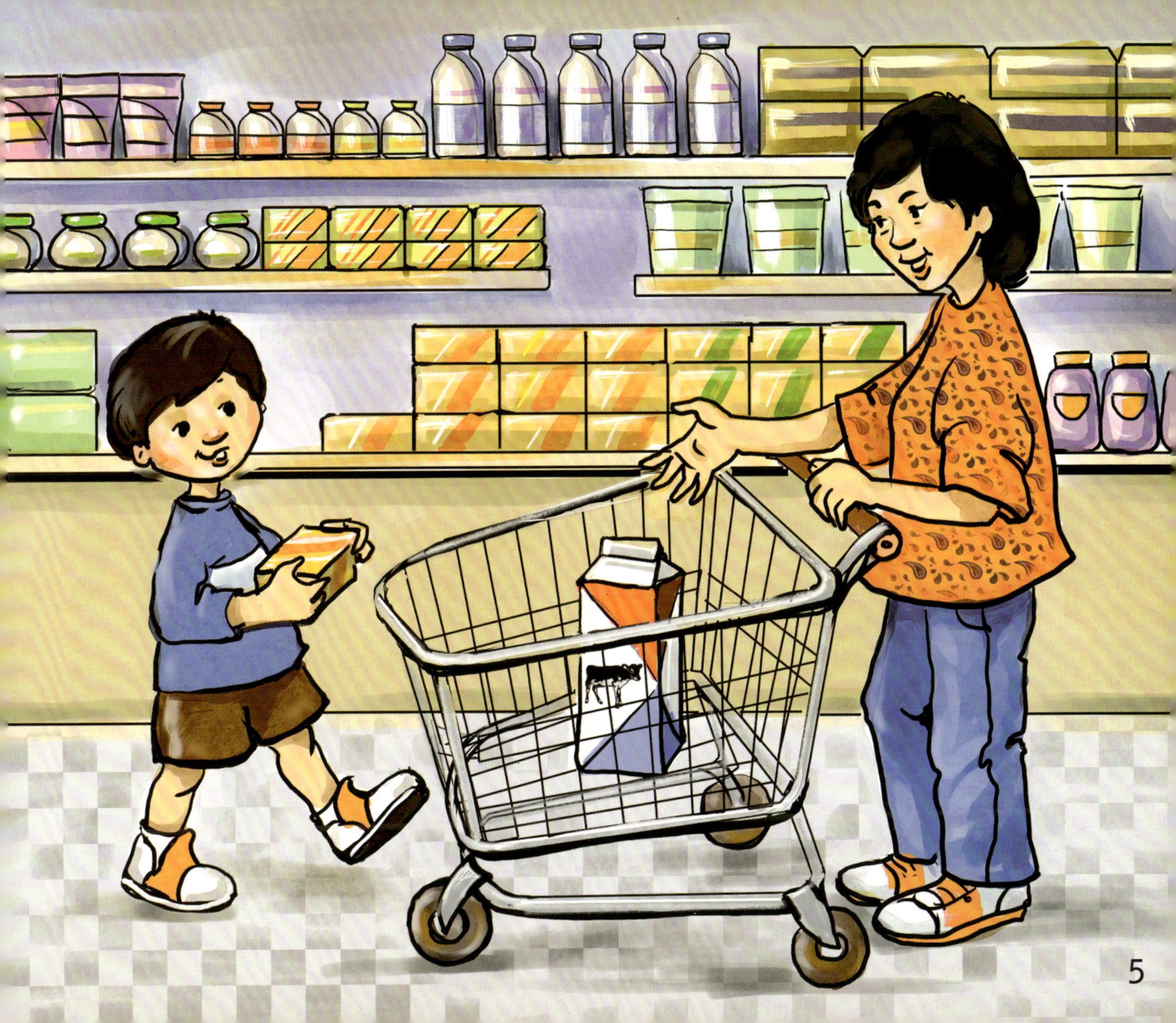

We get the meat.

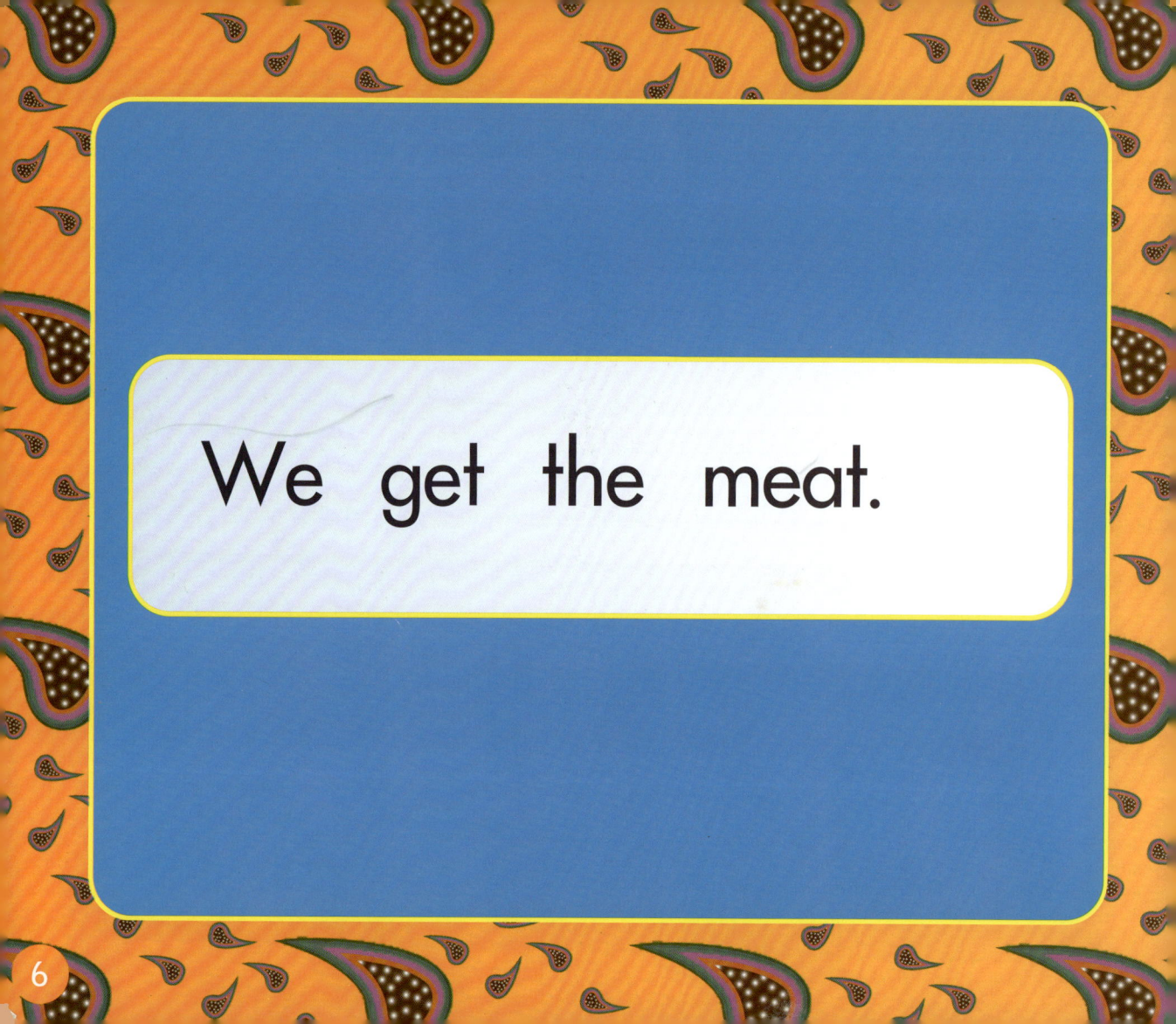

7

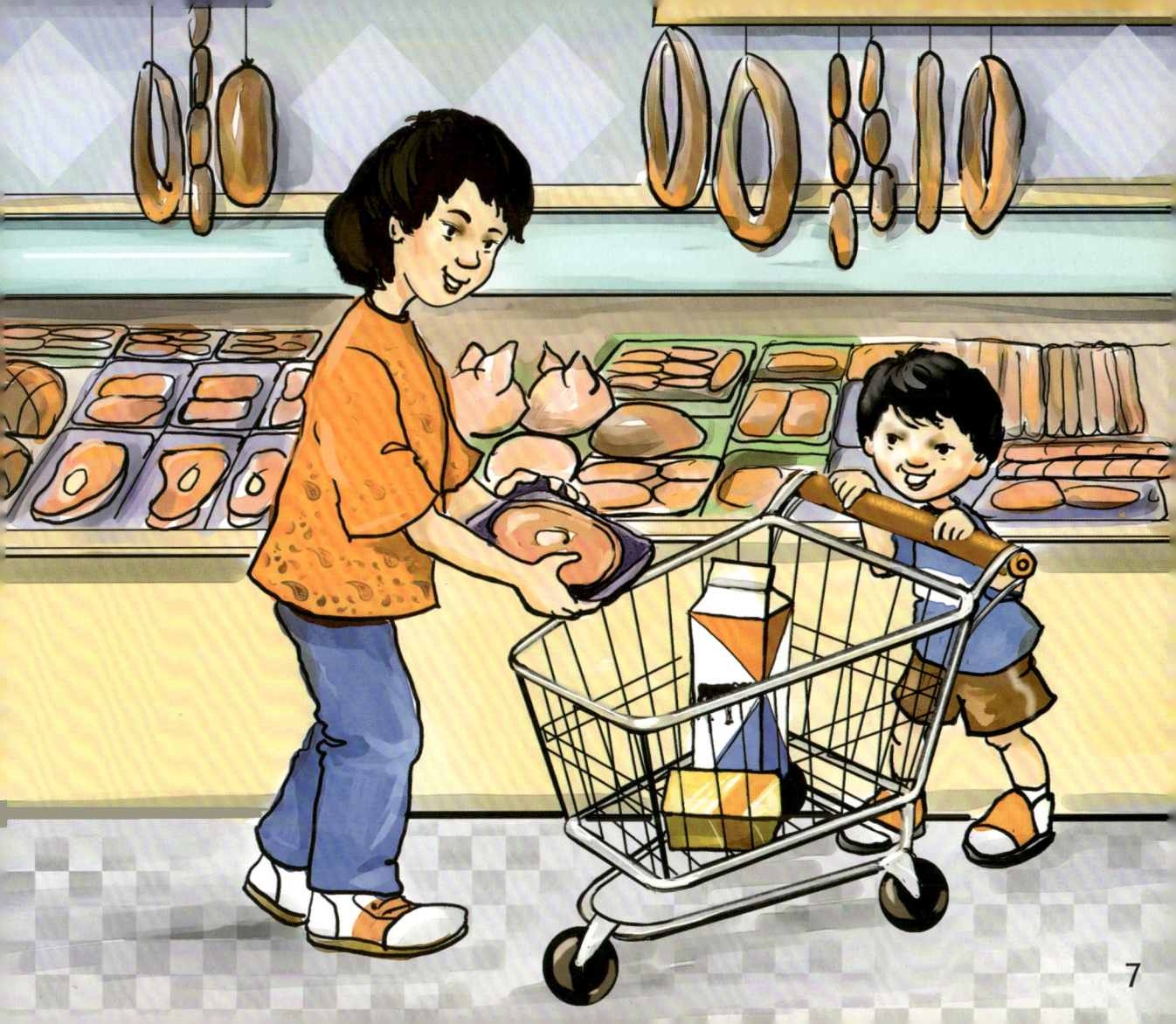

We get the bread.

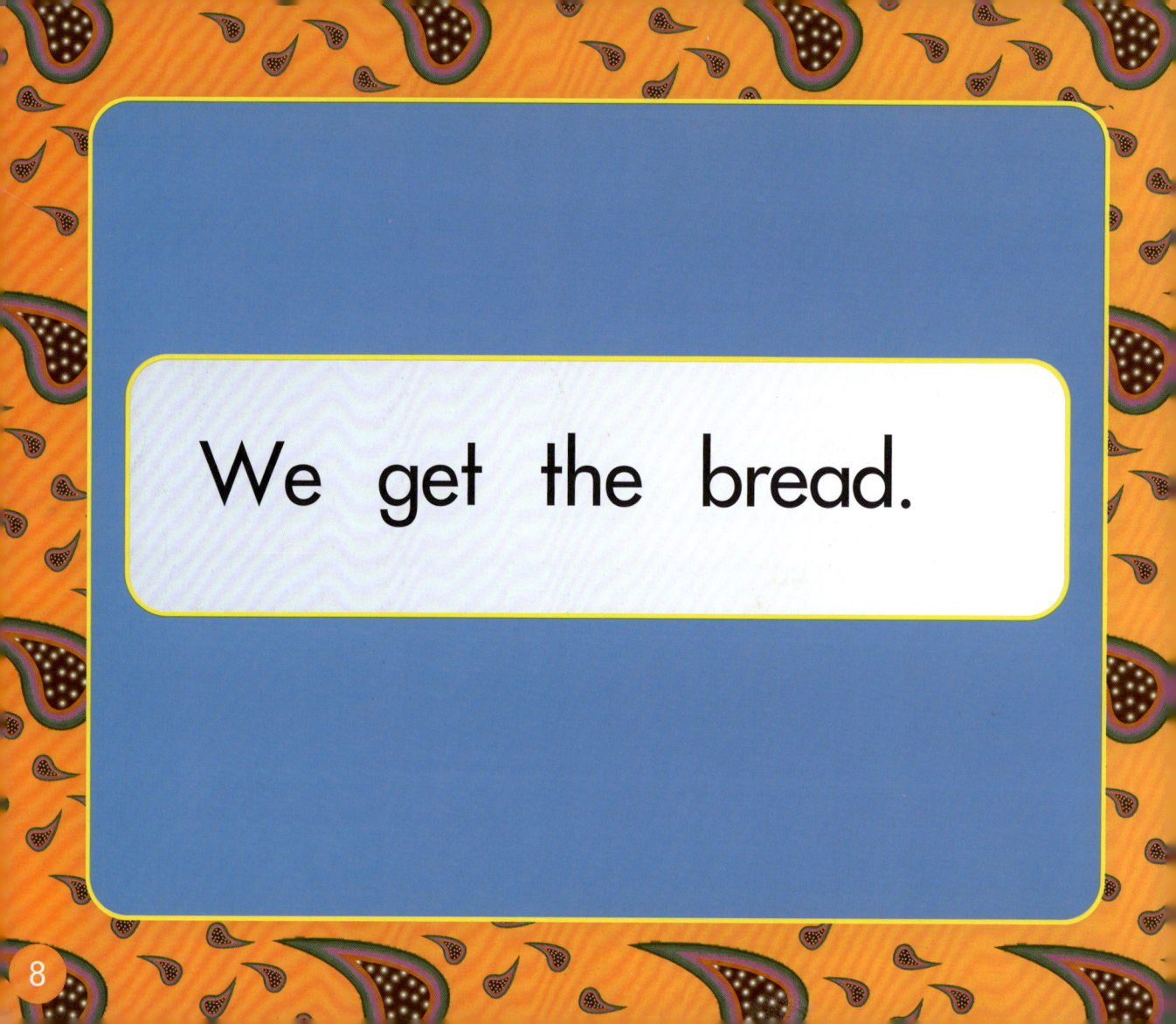

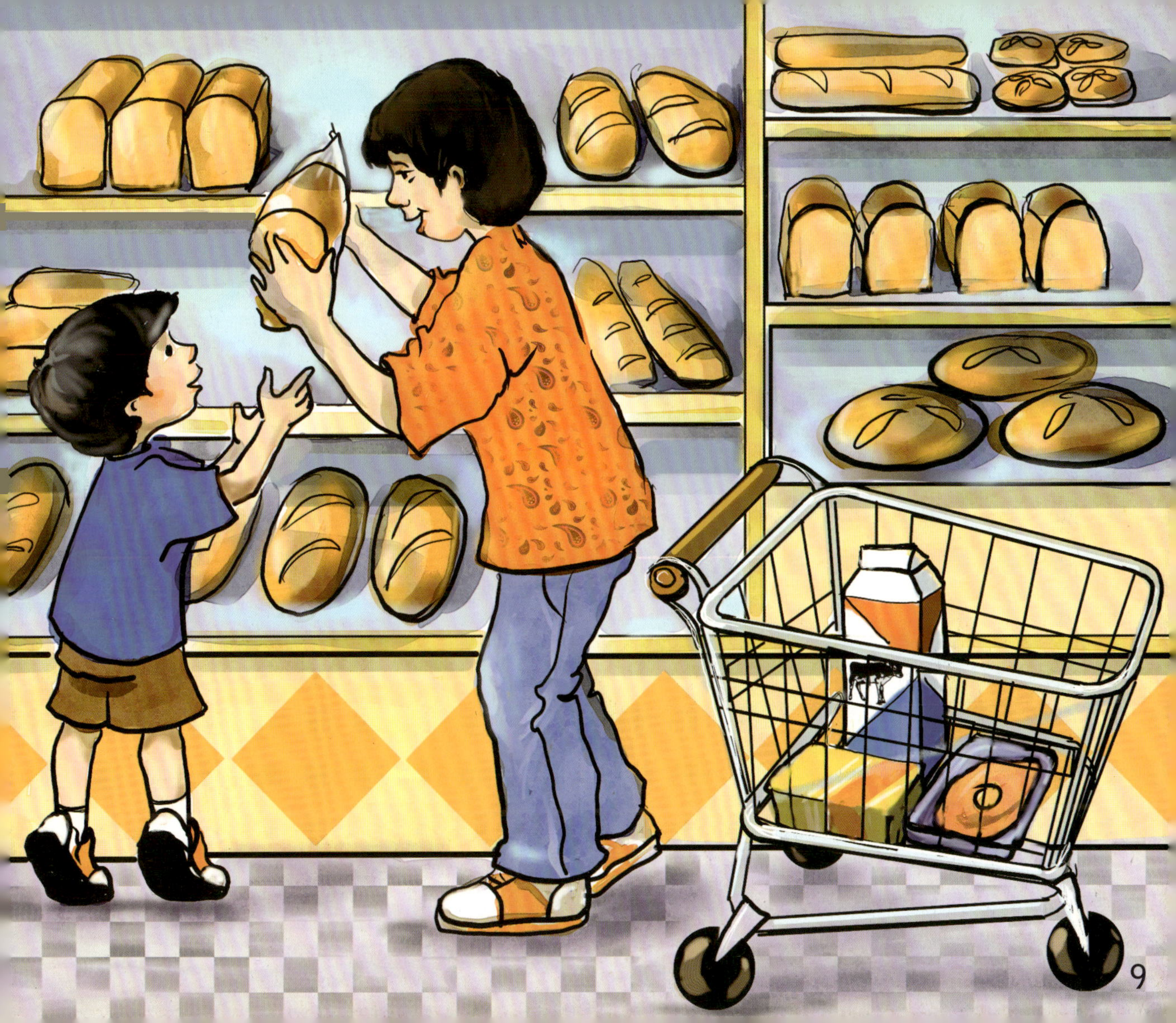

We get the jam.

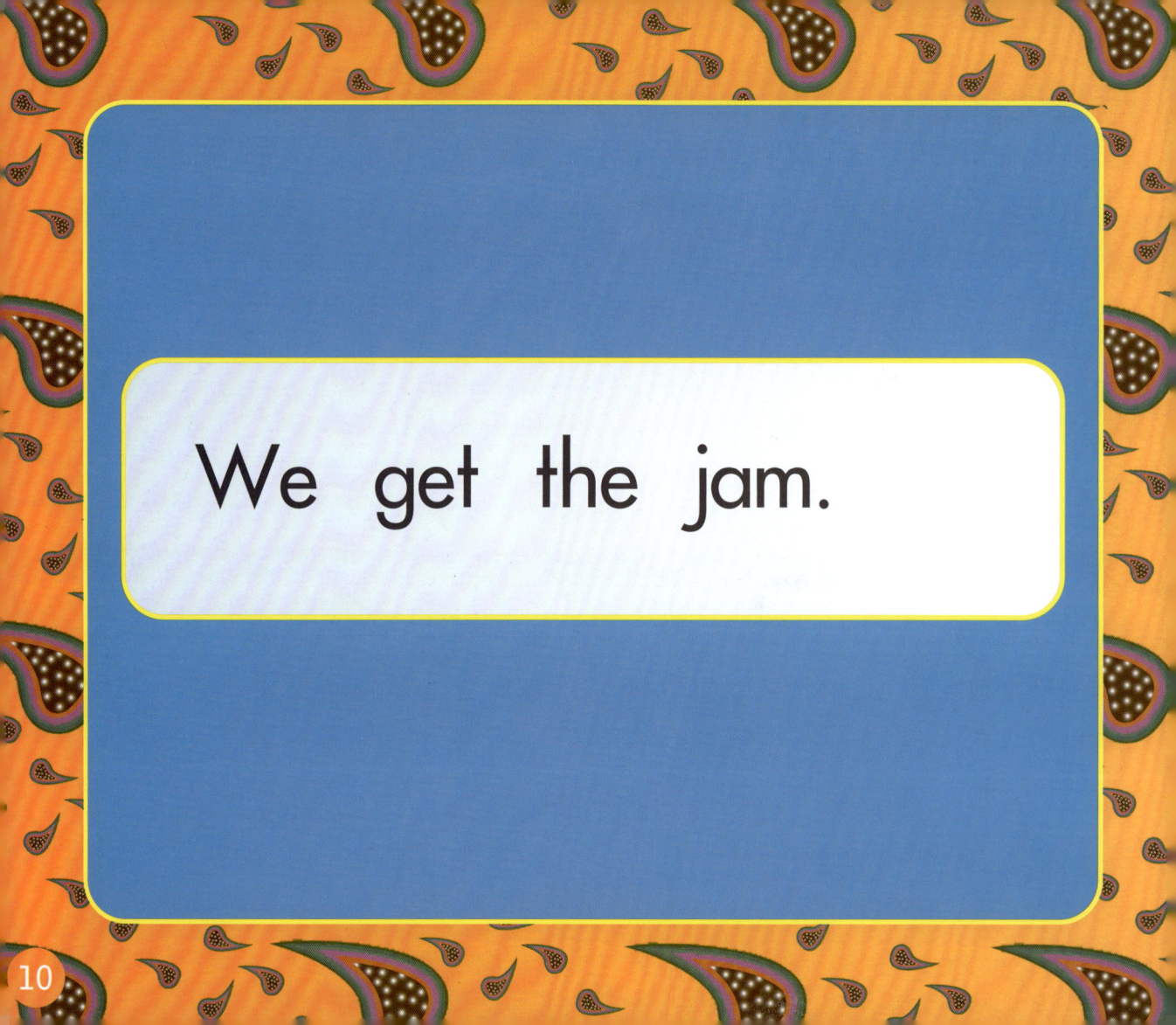

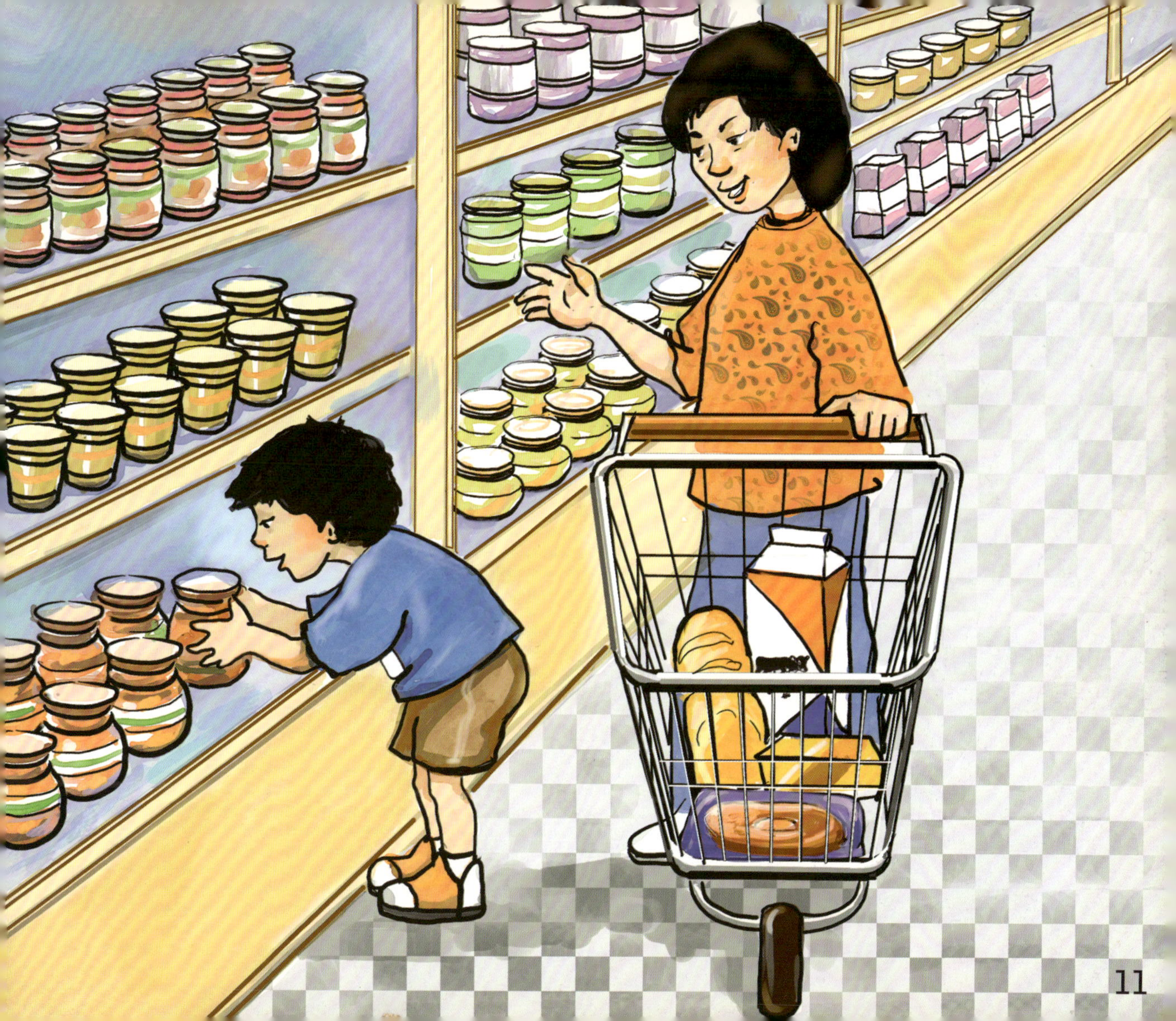

We get the bananas.

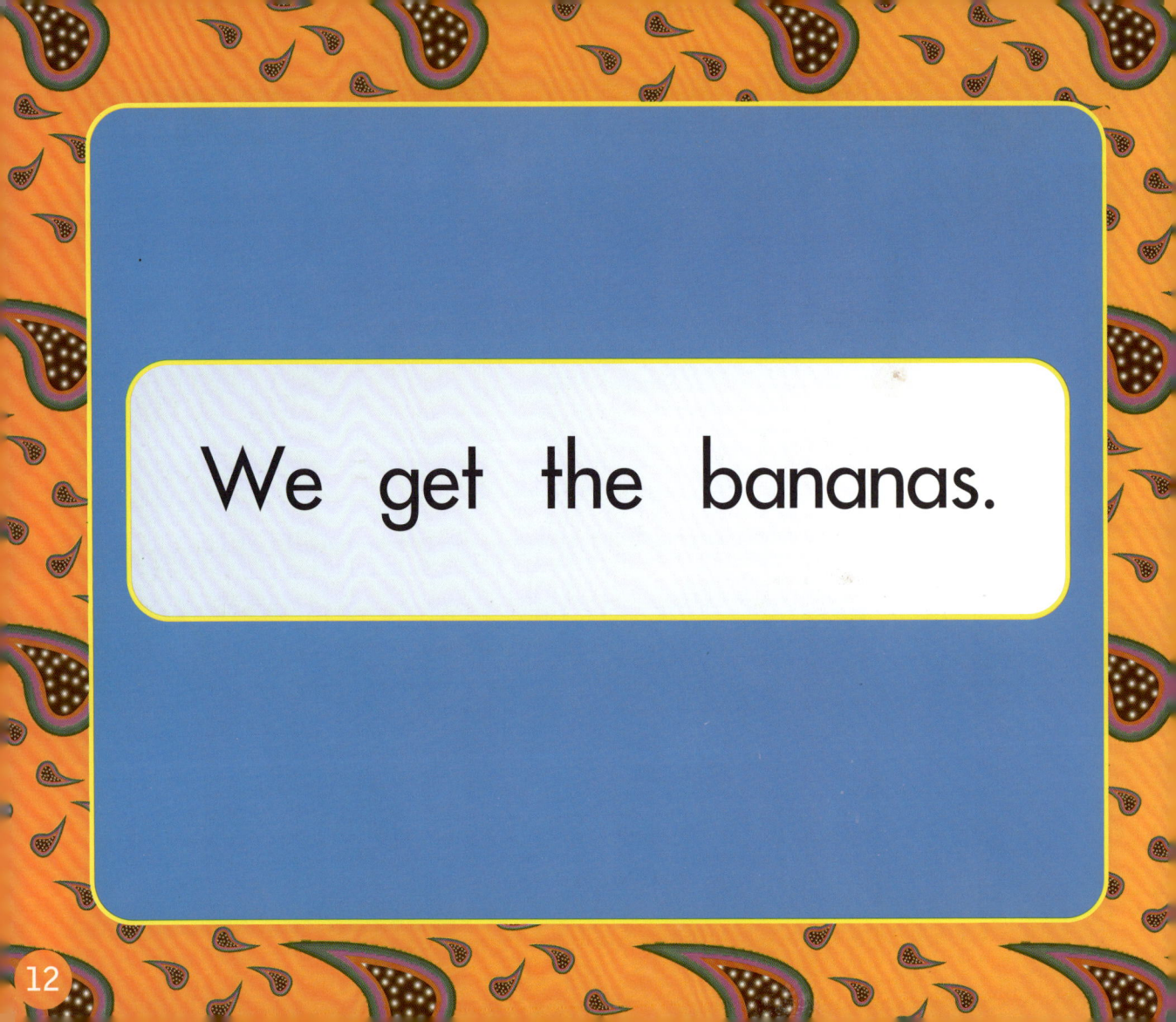

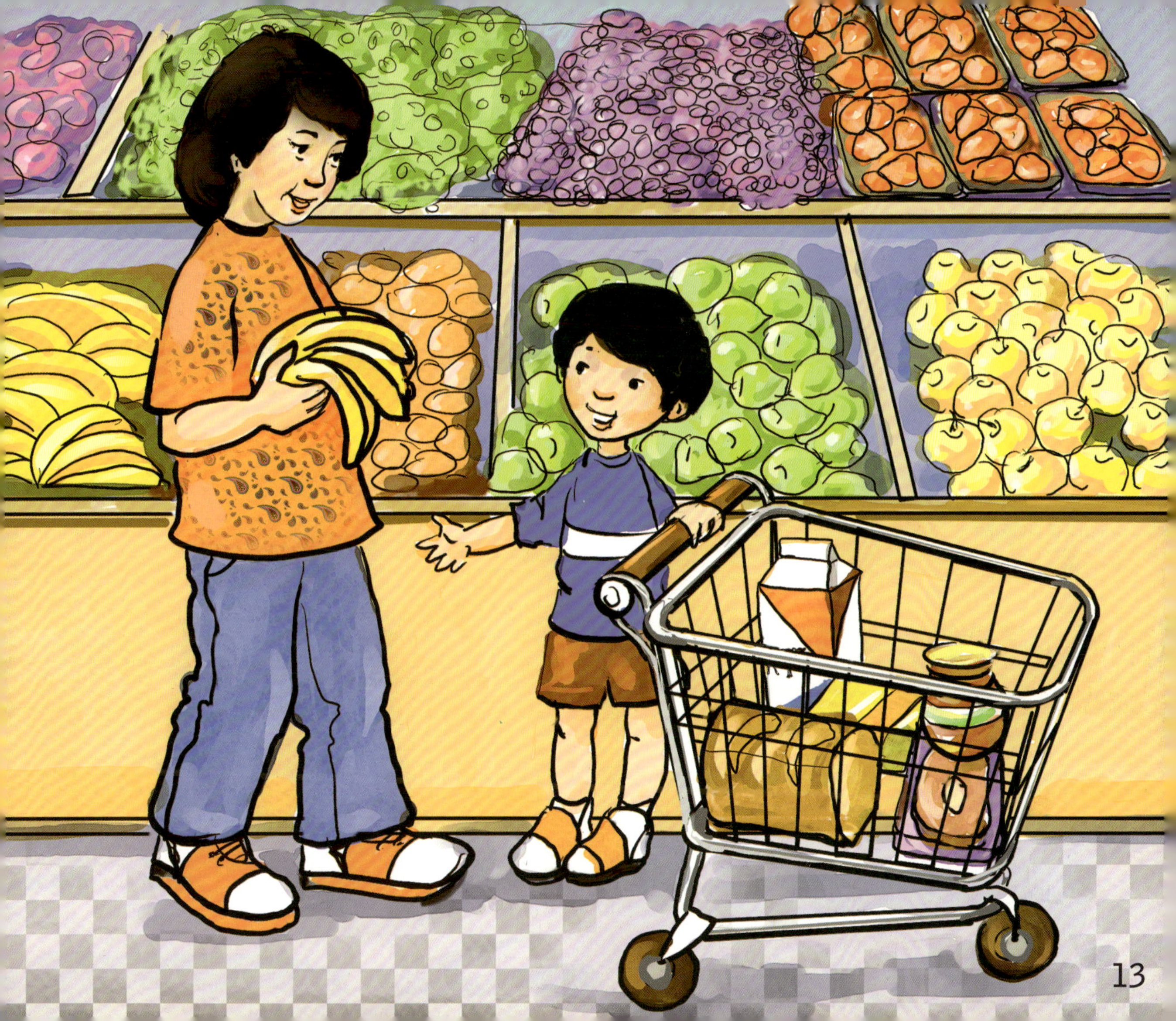

We get the carrots.

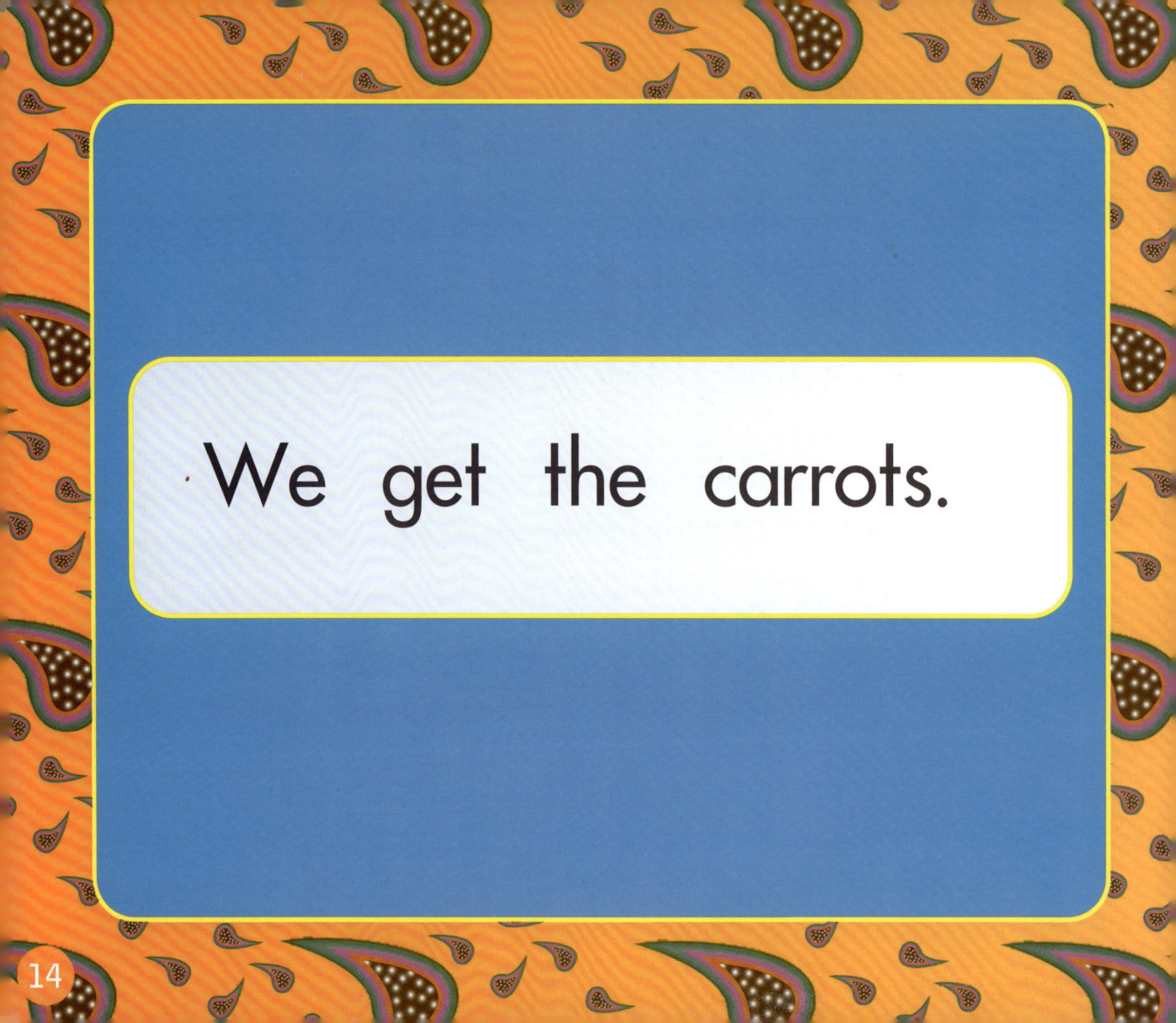

15

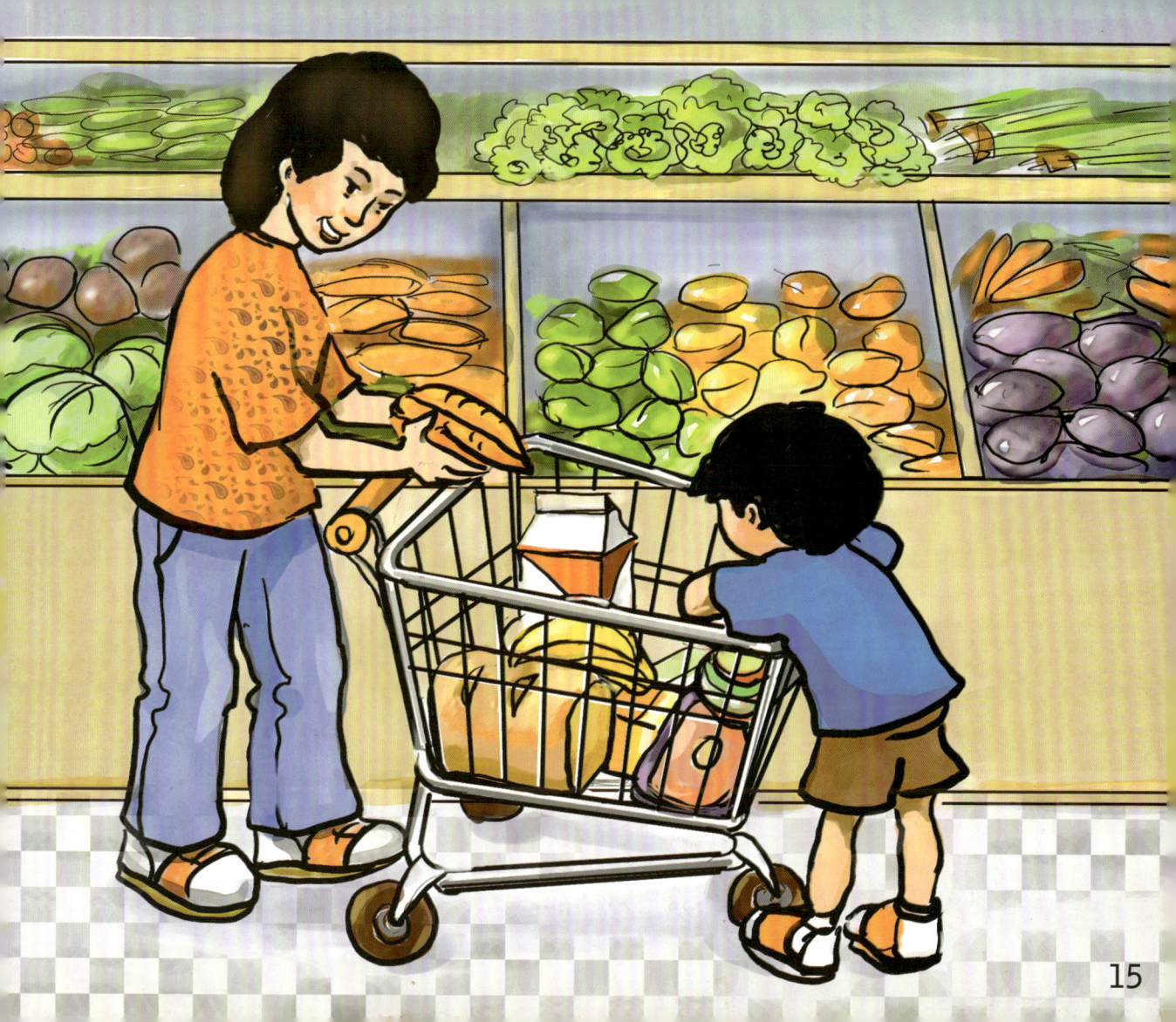

We get the bill!

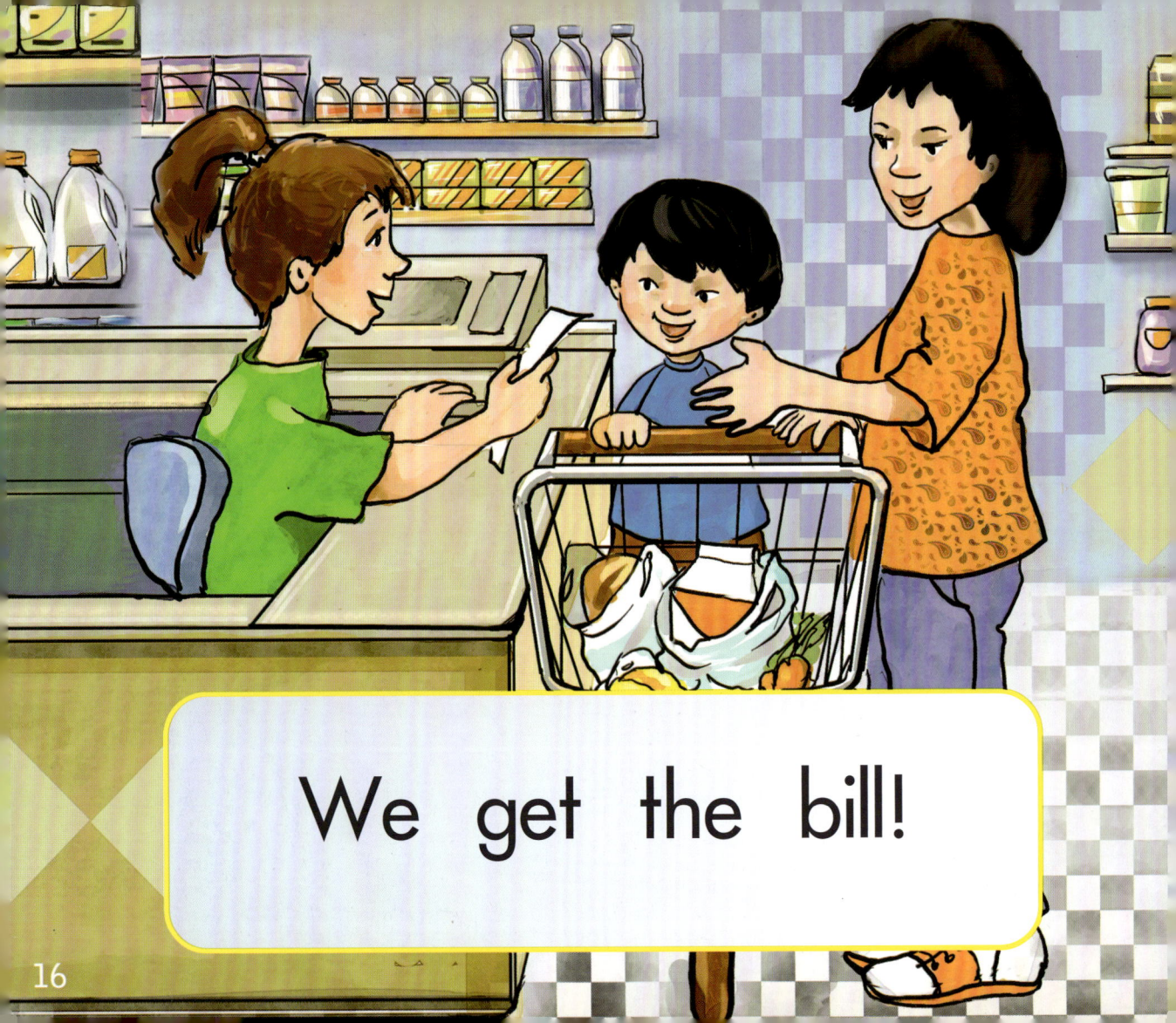